W9-DIM-446

THE POLITICS OF KING LEAR

THE POLITICS OF
KING LEAR

*The Seventh W. P. Ker Memorial Lecture delivered
in the University of Glasgow
23rd April, 1946*

by

EDWIN MUIR

Director of the British Institute, Prague

HASKELL HOUSE PUBLISHERS Ltd.
Publishers of Scarce Scholarly Books
NEW YORK. N. Y. 10012
1970

First Published 1947

HASKELL HOUSE PUBLISHERS LTD.
Publishers of Scarce Scholarly Books
280 LAFAYETTE STREET
NEW YORK. N. Y. 10012

Library of Congress Catalog Card Number: 76-99171

Standard Book Number 8383-0055-3

Printed in the Unit·d States of America

THE POLITICS OF KING LEAR

DURING the past few weeks I have been reading every now and then the collected essays of the great teacher and scholar in whose memory these lectures are held. They delighted but daunted me; for the massive equipment of learning which is handled in them with such ease is far beyond my command. I have come to books when I could, in the intervals of a life spent on other things, many of them not of my choosing; books have not been my occupation. But I console myself with the thought that every critic however learned must—for he cannot help it— bring to his interpretation of works of imagination not only his reading, but his life, the experiences he has passed through, the emotions he has felt, the reflections he has made upon them, even the accidents and trivialities of every day, since they are all parts of life and help us therefore to comprehend the poet's image of life.

In what I say to-day I do not intend to touch upon the more profound aspects of *King Lear*, though I hope my argument may have some reference to them. I want to speak of the politics of the play, and these must naturally have some relation to Shakespeare's politics. That, of course, is a difficult problem, and a great deal has been written about it by critics ancient and modern, from Coleridge to the late John Palmer and Dr. Tillyard in his last two volumes. I shall not try to summarize the arguments of these writers. But one point is crucial, and has been brought up repeatedly, and I should like to say a few words about it. Briefly, it has been maintained that Shakespeare had no politics. Now this may be true in a sense, if it merely means that he cannot be put down either as a Conservative, or as a Liberal, or as a Socialist, or whatever the counterparts of these modern classifications were in his time. I shall not use these terms, or adopt Swinburne's opinion that *King Lear* is the work of Shakespeare the Socialist: Swinburne was speaking rhetorically. But a man may have political sense, and political sense of a high kind, without falling into any of these categories; for his mind, while working politically, may not think in terms of any of them. To say that Shakespeare had no politics—if one takes the statement seriously—can only mean that he had no conception of what is good in society; and to assert that would bring an immediate denial from everybody. It has been said that he was above the conflict; it would be more true to say that he was above the classification. For he had very strongly a conception of what is good in society, just as he had very strongly a sense of what is good in conduct. Professor Caroline Spurgeon demonstrates this in her analysis of the Histories; but it seems to me that the play in which it is most clearly evident is *King Lear*.

To understand the Tragedies and the Histories one has to keep in mind the historical background of Shakespeare's age. I cannot attempt to describe that background, and must indicate it in a sort of historical shorthand by enumerating a few dates. The Dissolution of the Monasteries, which rang the warning that the old medieval order was nearing its end, was completed in 1539, twenty-five years before Shakespeare's birth. *King Lear* was written round about 1605–6, six or seven years after the birth of Cromwell and forty-three before the execution of Charles I. In the interval between the first and the last of these dates the medieval world with its communal tradition was slowly dying, and the modern individualist world was bringing itself to birth. Shakespeare lived in that violent period of transition. The old world still echoed in his ears; he was aware of the new as we are aware of the future, that is as an inchoate, semi-prophetic dream. Now it seems to me that that dream, those echoes, fill *King Lear* and account for the sense of vastness which it gives us, the feeling that it covers a far greater stretch of time than can be explained by the action. The extreme age of the King brings to our minds the image of a civilization of legendary antiquity; yet that civilization is destroyed by a new generation which belongs to Shakespeare's own time, a perfectly up-to-date gang of Renaissance adventurers. The play contains, therefore, or has taken on, a significance which Shakespeare probably could not have known, but could only have felt, and without his being aware, he wrote in it the mythical drama of the transmutation of civilization. One is reminded of the scene in the second part of Goethe's *Faust*, where the temples of the ancient world change and crumble and rise again in the towering Gothic structures of the Middle Ages.

Of the great tragedies *King Lear* is the only one in which two ideas of society are directly confronted, and the old generation and the new are set face to face, each assured of its own right to power. *Macbeth* is a drama of murder and usurpation and remorse; it changes the succession of the crown and brings guilt upon the offender, the guilt showing that the old order is still accepted, and the old laws still valid, since Macbeth feels that he has done wrong, both as the killer of a man and the supplanter of a king. But Regan, Goneril and Cornwall never feel they have done wrong, and this is because they represent a new idea; and new ideas, like everything new, bring with them their own kind of innocence. *Hamlet*, although it deals with a dynastic and therefore a political problem, is essentially a personal drama, perhaps the most personal of them all: there is no relationship in *King Lear* so intensely intimate as that of Hamlet to his mother. Lear's own relation to his daughters is most nearly so; yet Goneril and Regan are curiously equal in his estimation, indeed almost interchangeable; he is willing to accept either if she will only take his part against her sister; and as if his rage had blotted out their very names, he confounds them indistinguishably in his curses upon his daughters; so that we feel that daughters have become to him some strange and monstrous species. To Goneril and Regan, on the other hand, he is hardly even a father, but merely an old man who thinks and feels in a way they cannot understand, and is a burden to them. The almost impersonal equivalence of the two women in their father's eyes gives a cast to the play which is not to be found in any of the others, and makes us feel, indeed, that Lear is

not contending with ordinary human beings but
with mere forces to which any human appeal is vain,
since it is not even capable of evoking a response.
He, the representative of the old, is confronted with
something brand new; he cannot understand it, and
it does not even care to understand him.

There is something more, then, than ingratitude
in the reaction of Lear's daughters, though the ingratitude, that " marble-hearted fiend ", strikes
most deeply into his heart. This something more is
their attitude to power, which is grounded on their
attitude to life. It is this, more than the ingratitude,
that estranges Lear from them. His appeals cannot
reach them, but, worse still, his mind cannot understand them, no matter how hard he tries. As this
attitude of his daughters violates all his ideas of the
nature of things, it seems to him against nature, so
that he can only cry out against them as " unnatural
hags ". " Unnatural " is the nearest he can come to
a definition of the unbridgable distance that divides
him from them; his real struggle is to annihilate that
distance, but he never succeeds; in his most intimate
conflict with them he never comes any closer to them.
When Regan shuts him out in the storm her action
is symbolical as well as practical. His daughters are
inside; he is outside. They are in two different
worlds.

The story of *King Lear* tells how an old man parts
his kingdom between his daughters when he feels no
longer able to rule. He retains to himself only

The name and all th' addition to a king,

and leaves to them and their husbands

> The sway, revenue, execution of the rest.

His daughters, having got what they want, that is the power, and not caring much for the name or the addition, turn against him. As daughters, their act is one of filial ingratitude; as princesses and vice-regents, it is an act of "revolt and flying off". These two aspects of their policy are inseparable; in turning against their father they subvert the kingdom; by the same deed they commit two crimes, one private and one public.

But there is a complication. . For Goneril and Regan's idea of rulership is different from their father's and so on the anguish caused by their ingratitude is piled the bewilderment of one who feels he is dealing with creatures whose notions are equally incomprehensible to his heart and his mind. In the later stages of the conflict it is the tortures of his mind that become the most unbearable, since they make the nature of things incomprehensible to him, and confound his ideas in a chaos from which the only escape is madness. The note of Lear's tragedy is to be found in another play:

> Chaos is come again.

The note of the play itself, the summary judgment on the whole action, is expressed in Albany's words:

> If that the heavens do not their visible spirits
> Send quickly down to tame these vile offences,
> It will come
> Humanity must perforce prey on itself,
> Like monsters of the deep.

Yet this is the world which Lear's two daughters and
Cornwall and Edmund and Oswald freely accept as
theirs; it is their idea of a brand new order; and the
play therefore deals not only with a conflict between
two daughters and their father, and two vice-regents
and their king, but with two conceptions of society.

In the new conception of society, that of Goneril
and Regan, Nature plays an important part; the
number of references to Nature in the play, almost
always as images of cruelty or horror, has often been
commented upon. Bradley in his book on Shake-
spearean Tragedy tries to make a list of the lower
animals which are mentioned in the drama, a list
which had afterwards to be completed by Professor
Spurgeon. " These references are broadcast through
the whole play ", he says, " as though Shakespeare's
mind were so busy with the subject that he could
hardly write a page without some allusion to it.
The dog, the horse, the cow, the sheep, the hog, the
lion, the bear, the wolf, the fox, the monkey, the
pole-cat, the civet-cat, the pelican, the owl, the crow,
the chough, the wren, the fly, the butterfly, the rat,
the mouse, the frog, the tadpole, the wall-newt, the
water-newt, the worm—I am sure I cannot have
completed the list, and some of them are mentioned
again and again. . . . Sometimes a person in the
drama is compared, openly or implicitly, with one of
them. Goneril is a kite; her ingratitude has a serpent tooth: she has struck her father most serpent-
like upon the very heart: her visage is wolfish: she
has tied sharp-toothed unkindness like a vulture on
her father's breast: for her husband she is a gilded

serpent: to Gloster her cruelty seems to have the fangs of a boar. She and Regan are dog-hearted: they are tigers, not daughters; each is an adder to the other; the flesh of each is covered with the fell of a beast. . . . As we read, the souls of all the beasts in turn seem to us to have entered the bodies of these mortals; horrible in their venom, savagery, lust, deceitfulness, sloth, cruelty, filthiness."

After looking on this picture of nature, turn to the first speech of Edmund, the mouthpiece of the new generation:

> Thou, Nature, art my goddess; to thy law
> My services are bound. Wherefore should I
> Stand in the plague of custom, and permit
> The curiosity of nations to deprive me,
> For that I am some twelve or fourteen moonshines
> Lag of a brother? Why bastard? wherefore base?
> When my dimensions are as well compact,
> My mind as generous, and my shape as true,
> As honest madam's issue? Why brand they us
> With base? with baseness? bastardy? base, base?
> Who in the lusty stealth of nature take
> More composition and fierce quality
> Than doth, within a dull, stale, tired bed,
> Go to the creating a whole tribe of fops,
> Got 'tween asleep and wake? Well then,
> Legitimate Edgar, I must have your land:
> Our father's love is to the bastard Edmund
> As to the legitimate. Fine word, ' legitimate '.

Goneril and Regan and Cornwall, though they do not have Edmund's imaginative intellect, worship Nature in the same spirit. For it gives them the freedom they hunger for, absolves them from the plague of custom, justifies them when they reflect that their dimensions are well-compact and their shape true, as if that were all that was needed to make human a creature in human shape. They rely confidently on certain simple facts of nature: that they are young and their father old, strong while he is infirm, and that their youth and strength give them a short-cut to their desires. They are so close to the state of nature that they hardly need to reflect: what they have the power to do they claim the right to do. Or rather the power and its expression in action are almost simultaneous. When Lear pleads with Goneril she replies:

> Be then desir'd
> By her that else will take the thing she begs
> A little to disquantity your train.

Regan says a little later:

> I pray you, father, being weak, seem so.

After Cornwall puts out Gloster's eyes and Regan stabs the servant who tried to prevent it, he says:

> Turn out that eyeless villain; throw this slave
> Upon the dunghill.

And Regan adds,

> Go thrust him out at gates, and let him *smell*
> His way to Dover.

The most repulsive thing about these words, apart from their cruelty, is their triteness. The two daughters ignore all the complexities of the situation, and solve it at once by an abominable truism. They are quite rational, but only on the lowest plane of reason, and they have that contempt for other

ways of thinking which comes from a knowledge of
their own efficiency. As they are rational, they have
a good conscience, even a touch of self-righteousness;
they sincerely believe their father is in the wrong and
they are in the right, since they conceive they know
the world as it is, and act in conformity with it, the
source of all effective power. They do not see far,
but they see clearly. When they reflect, and take
thought for the future, their decisions are rational
and satisfactory by their own standards. When
Goneril wants an excuse for reducing her father's
retinue, she instructs her servant Oswald how to
behave towards him:

> Put on what weary negligence you please,
> You and your fellows : I'd have it come to question . . .
> And let his knights have colder looks among you;
> What grows of it, no matter: advise your fellows so:
> I would breed from hence occasions, and I shall,
> That I may speak.

This is a technique which we have seen much prac-
tised in our own time.

The members of the new generation are bound
together by common interest, since they all wish to
succeed in their individual ambitions, which they cannot achieve without help; but their most immediate
bond is a common way of thinking, a spontaneous
intellectual affinity resembling that of a chosen
group to whom a new vision of the world has been
vouchsafed. They feel they are of the elect and have
the sense of superiority which fits their station.
They are irresistibly driven to choose as confederates
men and women of their own stamp, even though

these are likely in the long run to thwart or destroy them. Having renounced morality as a useful factor in conduct, they judge others with a total lack of moral discrimination, being confined irretrievably to the low plane of reason on which they move. Accordingly Cornwall can say to Edmund:

> You shall be ours;
> Natures of such deep trust we shall much need;
> You we first seize on.

And of honest Kent:

> This is some fellow,
> Who, having been praised for bluntness, doth affect
> A saucy roughness, and constrains the garb
> Quite from his nature: he cannot flatter, he;
> An honest man and plain, he must speak truth:
> An they will have it, so; if not, he's plain.
> These kind of rogues I know, which in this plainness
> Harbour more craft and more corrupter ends
> Than twenty silly-ducking observants
> That stretch their duties nicely.

Lear could not have made these mistakes, for he had some knowledge of the moral nature of men; but Cornwall and Goneril and Regan can and do; for while they have worked out the equation of life with complete satisfaction to themselves, they have done so by omitting the moral factor.

The new generation may be regarded then as the embodiment of wickedness, a wickedness of that special kind which I have tried to indicate. But can it also be said that they represent a new conception of society? If we had not lived through the last twenty years, had not seen the rise of Fascism in

Italy and Germany, and did not know the theory and practice by which it was upheld, we might be disposed to deny this. As it is we cannot. We know, too, that Shakespeare was acquainted with the Renaissance man, and that his plays abound in references to " policy ", which stood in his time for what the Germans dignify by the name of *Realpolitik*, that is political action which ignores all moral considerations. In Burckhardt's account of the lives of the Roman condottieri there is ground enough for believing that figures like Goneril and Regan could both behave as they did and rule a state. It was an age in which Italian princes, and others too, permitted themselves a liberty of action which one would have expected to disrupt or destroy the state; yet it did not. Instead, the subject conformed to a rulership which itself seemed impossible because antisocial; he conformed by becoming the mere instrument of his ruler. The Macchiavellian became a stock figure in later Elizabethan drama; Shakespeare must have met many a man like Edmund who refused to be deprived by the plague of custom. Bradley calls Edmund a mere adventurer, yet afterwards describes him as a consummate politician in the new style. " He acts in pursuance of a purpose ", says Bradley, " and if he has any affections or dislikes, ignores them. He is determined to make his way, first to his brother's lands, then—as the prospect widens—to the crown; and he regards men and women, with their virtues and vices, together with the bonds of kinship, friendship, or allegiance, merely as hindrances or helps to his end. They are for him divested of all quality except their relation to his end; as indifferent as mathematical quantities or mere physical agents.

> A credulous father and a brother noble,
> . . . I see the business,

he says, as if he were talking of x and y."

To regard things in this way is to see them in a continuous present divested of all associations, denuded of memory and the depth which memory gives to life. Goneril and Regan, even more than Edmund, exist in this shallow present, and it is to them a present in both senses of the word, a gift freely given into their hands to do with what they like. Having no memory, they have no responsibility, and no need therefore to treat their father differently from any other troublesome old man. This may simply be another way of saying that they are evil, for it may be that evil consists in a hiatus in the soul, a craving blank, a lack of one of the essential threads which bind experience into a coherent whole and give it a consistent meaning. The hiatus in Lear's daughters is specifically a hiatus of memory, a breach in continuity; they seem to come from nowhere and to be on the road to nowhere; they have words and acts only to meet the momentary emergency, the momentary appetite; their speech is therefore strikingly deficient in imagery, and consists of a sequence of pitiless truisms. Bradley complains of the characters in the play that, " Considered simply as psychological studies few of them are of the highest interest." This is true of Goneril and

Regan, for the human qualities of highest interest are left out of them. But this was Shakespeare's intention; he had to interest us in two characters who were both evil and shallow. Their shallowness is ultimately that of the Macchiavellian view of life as it was understood in his age, of " policy ", or *Realpolitik*, whichever we may choose to call it. The sisters are harpies, but as rulers they act in the approved contemporary Macchiavellian convention. If we read Burckhardt, if we reflect that Macchiavellianism was a current preoccupation in Shakespeare's time, and consider further that the Renaissance gave to the individual a prominence he had not possessed since classical times, and that personal power, especially in princes, appeared sometimes to be boundless, we need not shrink from regarding Edmund and his confederates as political types. Poets of Shakespeare's time had espoused the liberated hero, the glorious individual, among them Marlowe, and Chapman with his ideal of " royal man ". But Shakespeare did not: his political sense put him on the opposite side.

To understand his attitude to the new generation we must finally consider his identification of them with nature. Their life in the moment, their decisions based on what the mere moment presents, their want of continuity, their permanent empty newness, are sufficient in themselves to involve them with nature, for nature is always new and has no background: it is society that is old. Their position may be defined by saying that they claim a liberty which is proper to nature but not to society. This is

what makes them in a sense unnatural; and this is
what makes it impossible for Lear with his traditional
beliefs to understand them. Nature is not corrupt in
itself, nor is man as Shakespeare normally sees him;
but when man is swallowed up in nature a result is
produced which seems to corrupt both. Goneril,
Regan and Cornwall become mere animals furnished
with human faculties which they have stolen, not
inherited by right. Words are their teeth and claws,
and action the technique of the deadly spring.
It may be that this new freedom, the freedom of
nature not of civilised humanity, pointed to the
development which society was to follow, to
laissez-faire and the struggle for existence and the
survival of the fittest so dear to the Victorian econo-
mists: but I have no time to follow it there.

Against this idea of society what had Lear to set?
His conception is nowhere clearly formulated, for it
is old, and it is to him the accepted conception. But
in almost everything he says, whether in anger or
kindness, we can feel what it is: he sets against the
idea of natural freedom the sacred tradition of human
society. His attitude to nature when he is in his
right mind is quite objective:

> Allow not nature more than nature needs,
> Man's life is cheap as beast's :

He himself does not turn to nature for help until his
folly is let in and his dear judgement out, and then he
asks her, the terrible goddess, to fulfil his curse on
Goneril:

> If she must teem
> Create her child of spleen, that it may live
> To be a thwart disnatur'd torment to her.
> Let it stamp wrinkles on her brow of youth,
> With cadent tears fret channels in her cheeks,
> Turn all her mother's pains and benefits
> To laughter and contempt, that she may find
> How sharper than a serpent's tooth it is
> To have a thankless child.

Later, when his mind is tortured by the problem of his daughters' insensibility, his speculations on nature take on a darker colour:

> Then let them anatomize Regan, see what breeds about her heart. Is there any cause in nature that makes these hard hearts?

The more forlorn his state becomes, the more he feels the indifference and cruelty of nature even in small things:

> The little dogs and all, ⁃
> Tray, Blanche, and Sweet-heart, see, they bark
> at me.

He sees clearly what man is in his natural state, and describes him after he meets Edgar in his rags:

> Is man no more than this? Consider him well. Thou owest the worm no silk, the beast no hide, the sheep no wool, the cat no perfume. Ha! here's three on's are sophisticated: thou art the thing itself; unaccommodated man is no more than such a poor bare, forked animal as thou art.

Yet for Lear and his friends there exists an order of society so obviously springing from the nature and needs of man that it can also be called natural, though not in Edmund's sense. When it is subverted, the universal frame seems to be wrenched from its place, and the new chaos can be explained only as the result of a portent. Gloster argues:

These late eclipses in the sun and moon portend no good to us: though the wisdom of nature can argue it thus and thus, yet nature finds itself scourged by the sequent effects. Love cools, friendship falls off, brothers divide: in cities, mutinies: in countries, discord: in palaces, treason: and the bond cracked between son and father. . . . We have seen the best of our time: machinations, hollowness, treachery, and all ruinous disorders follow us disquietly to our graves.

Kent exclaims:

It is the stars,
The stars above us, govern our conditions;
Else one self mate and make could not beget
Such different conditions.

Gloster and Kent needed such explanations, for division between brothers, mutinies, discords, teacheries, did not seem to them in accordance with the nature of society. But to Edmund this state is the natural one, for it gives him an opportunity to rise; and so he can sneer almost virtuously at his father's superstitions:

This is the excellent foppery of the world, that, when we are sick in fortune,—often the surfeit of our own behaviour, —we make guilty of our disasters the sun, the moon, and the stars; as if we were villains by necessity, fools by heavenly compulsion, knaves, thieves, and treachers by spherical predominance, drunkards, liars, and adulterers by an enforced obedience of planetary influence; and all that we are evil in, by a divine thrusting on: an admirable evasion of whoremaster man, to lay his goatish disposition to the charge of a star! My father compounded with my mother under the dragon's tail, and my nativity was under *ursa major;* so that it follows I am rough and lecherous. 'Sfoot, I should have been that I am, had the maidenliest star in the firmament t⸳⸳ⁿkled on my bastardizing.

Edmund can say this because he is a child of nature, and a liar, adulterer and treacher by free choice, for each furthers his advancement.

The tradition of society which Lear represents is difficult to reconstruct from anything that is said in the play. Its nature is implied in Lear's appeals to his daughters:

> 'Tis not in thee
> To grudge my pleasures, to cut off my train,
> To bandy hasty words, to scant my sizes,
> And, in conclusion, to oppose the bolt
> Against my coming in: thou better know'st
> The offices of nature, bond of childhood,
> Effects of courtesy, dues of gratitude.

It is to such things that Lear appeals when he is trying to find a way to his daughters; not to interest or advantage. He appeals to a sentiment which to him means everything, but which to them means nothing: they do not even understand it. His conception of society can be guessed at again in the words which he says to his Fool out of his own grief:

> Poor fool and knave, I have one part in my heart
> That's sorry yet for thee.

We can guess at it again in these words which made Swinburne write of Shakespeare the Socialist:

> Poor naked wretches, wheresoe'er you are,
> That bide the pelting of this pitiless storm,
> How shall your houseless heads and unfed sides,

> Your loop'd and window'd raggedness, defend you
> From seasons such as these? O, I have ta'en
> Too little care of this. Take physic, pomp;
> Expose thyself to feel what wretches feel,
> That thou mayst shake the superflux to them,
> And show the heavens more just.

The difference between that and

> I pray you, father, being weak, seem so,

or

> Go thrust him out at gates, and let him smell
> His way to Dover,

is the difference between the two worlds described in the play. Lear is an imperfect king; he has taken too little care for his subjects; but he admits the obligation; and the social realities on which he relies, and to which he appeals as if they were self-evident, are purely human, not realistic in the modern sense:

> The offices of nature, bond of childhood,
> Effects of courtesy, dues of gratitude.

If we discern a conception of society behind such fragmentary utterances, and behind Lear himself, it appears to us as a society bound together not by force and appetite, but by a sort of piety and human fitness, a natural piety, one would feel inclined to say, if the word were not used in the play as inimical to society.

Lear is very old, almost Saturnian in his legendary age; the kingdom in him exists as a memory and no longer as a fact; the old order lies in ruin, and the new is not an order. The communal tradition, filled with memory, has been smashed by an individualism that exists in its perpetual shallow present. The judgement on the new generation is passed by a member of it who does not belong spiritually to it: Edgar. It is remarkable that in the scenes where Lear, the Fool and Edgar are together, it is Edgar, the only sane man, who conjures up the deepest images of horror. For he is of the new generation, and knows it as Lear cannot. When Lear asks him who he is, he replies by giving a portrait of his brother Edmund:

A serving-man, proud in heart and mind; that curled my hair; wore gloves in my cap; served the lust of my mistress' heart and did the act of darkness with her; swore as many oaths as I spake words and broke them in the sweet face of heaven: one that slept in the contriving of lust and waked to do it: wine loved I deeply, dice dearly, and in woman out-paramoured the Turk: false of heart, light of ear, bloody of hand: hog in sloth, fox in stealth, wolf in greediness, lion in prey.

That is a picture of an animal with human faculties, made corrupt and legendary by the proudly curled hair. It is a picture, too, of the man of policy in the latest style, who regards the sacred order of society as his prey, and recognizes only two realities, interest and force, the gods of the new age.